THIS BOOK BELONGS TO

_____

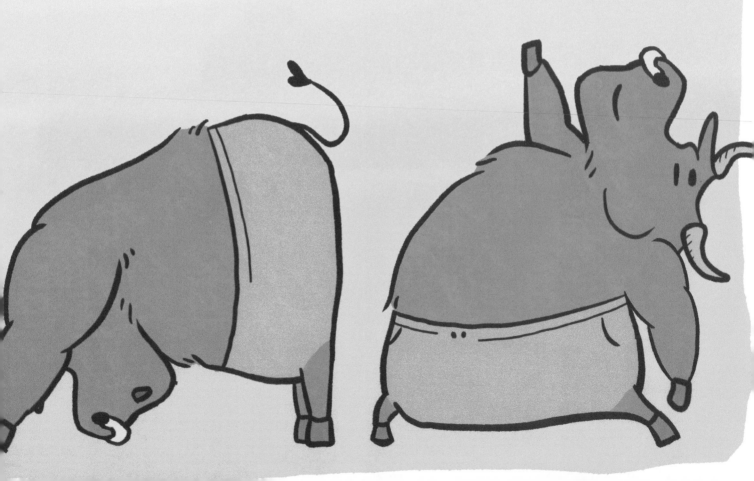

Bull was a master of zen. When bad things happened, he never seemed angry or anxious, and always had positive things to say. No one had ever seen him in a bad mood!

So he just went shopping again, whistling all the way.
Onions, peppers, beans, and garlic.

This second time, his chili was even more delicious than before. Everyone at the picnic loved it! There is always a silver lining to each cloud.

Another time, Bull broke his favorite robot action figure. Bull was upset, but he shrugged his horns and said

And just the day before, Bull didn't make his school's basketball team. Most people would be quite sad about this.

Bull was indeed sad, but he knew he'd just have more time to practice watercolor painting!

Bull was the very definition of even-keeled, positive, and calm. He began to be called by the nickname, Buddha. But Bull had come a very long way to deal with his anger and negativity so calmly.

Bull used to be very angry. At anything small, he would blow up and be unable to control his anger. He would scream, shout, and kick about.

The worst part about this was that Bull's family and friends hated it. He scared them! And they didn't want to spend very much time with him. He just wasn't very fun.

Duck ended up telling Fox about Bull's problem, and Fox came over to Bull's house with some cookies.

Fox had an idea for Bull, and it was all about remaining calm and zen whenever something bad happened. "I just used it last week when I skinned my knee!"

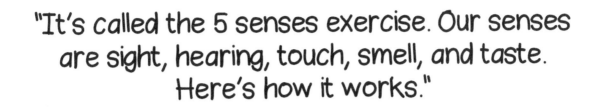

"The tough part is to replace the habit of getting angry, with the habit of the 5 senses exercise and staying calm and zen! If 5 is too much to remember, just start with seeing and hearing."

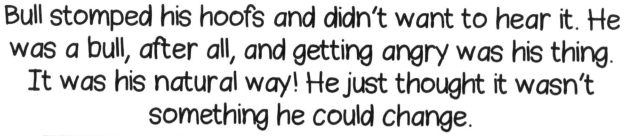

Bull stomped his hoofs and didn't want to hear it. He was a bull, after all, and getting angry was his thing. It was his natural way! He just thought it wasn't something he could change.

But if he just kept doing the same thing, he would just get the same result. So he decided to try. The following week, Giraffe made fun of Bull for not making the school basketball team.

He was about to explode, but he knew there was another way. So he starting looking for 5 things to see, 4 to hear, 3 to feel, 2 to smell, and 1 to taste.

And do you know what happened?

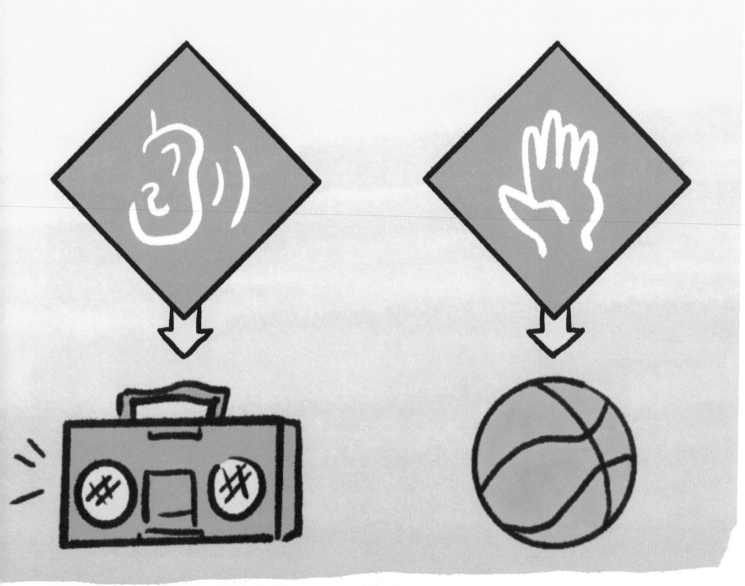

Bull got so focused on naming 3 things to feel that he completely forgot about Giraffe! He forgot his angry emotion, and he finished the exercise. He was suddenly calm and thoughtful, and not angry at all.

Bull didn't even realize until later on that it worked so well, and that it wasn't difficult at all! Bull was so excited he did a twirl on his horns.

The next day, Bull spilled red paint all over his new white backpack! At first, he wanted to cry! But he remembered the 5 senses exericse. 5 things to see, 4 to hear, 3 to feel, 2 to smell, and 1 to taste...

And just like the day before, it worked like a charm. He focused on something besides his anger and stayed calm the entire time. It was within his control!

Bull had seen enough to be convinced. From that day on, whenever Bull felt a bit of anger rising in his head, he started the 5 senses exercise. And eventually he didn't have the habit of getting angry anymore and always remained calm and thoughtful.

The 5 senses exercise might just be your secret weapon too: to remain relaxed and in control of your emotions. Your friends will love you!

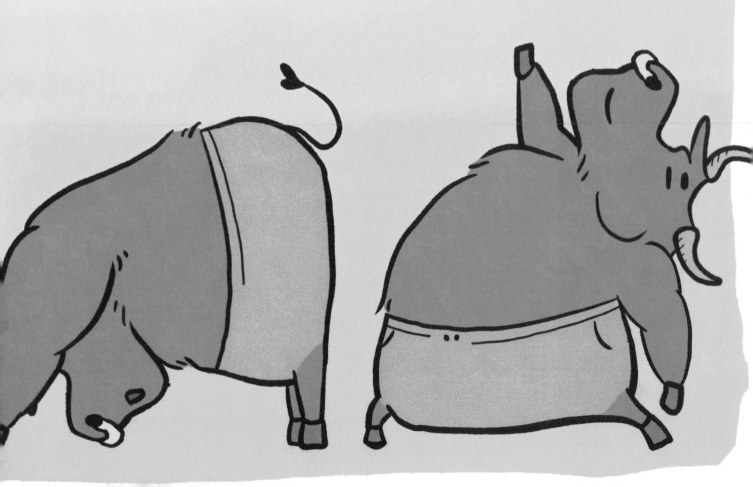

Visit Big Barn Press BigBarnPress.com to see free printable downloads, upcoming releases, and the rest of our catalog

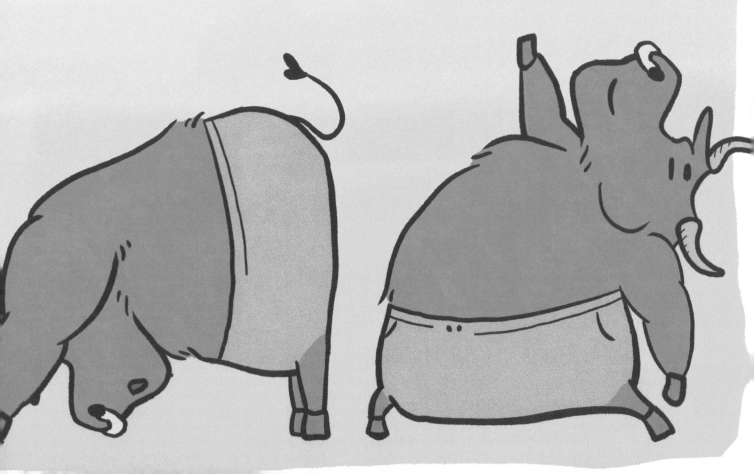

CPSIA information can be obtained
at www.ICGtesting.com
Printed in the USA
LVHW071331040621
689378LV00007B/382